what is ISLAM ?

ANSWERS TO THE MOST
COMMONLY ASKED QUESTIONS

First Edition, 2018

Revised Second Edition, 2019

British Library Cataloguing-in-Publication Data

A catalogue record for this book is available from the British Library

ISBN: 978-1-9164041-1-3

Compiled by: British Muslim Heritage Centre

Published by: BMHC

                               Email: info@bmhc.org.uk

                               Website: www.bmhc.org.uk

BRITISH MUSLIM HERITAGE CENTRE

Contents

Contents

Contents

Contents

In The Name of God,
The Most Merciful, The Most Beneficent

Foreword

Islam is the religion and way of life for almost 25% of the world's population.[1] There is hardly a place in the world today where Islam is entirely unknown, or where Muslims are not present. Muslims are of diverse nationalities, cultures, and races, and a growing number of people have become curious enough to seek knowledge about this widely publicised religion; more often than not, they have been pleasantly surprised. In contemporary societies, particularly in the West, Islam is generally misunderstood and Muslims are being stigmatised and are facing a number of challenges, including Islamophobia. Therefore, it is hoped this booklet will help shed some light on Islam and dispel many of the prevailing misconceptions.

With this objective in mind, the British Muslim Heritage Centre (BMHC) presents a brief overview of Islam, with answers to some of the most commonly asked questions. Therefore, it is a great honour for me to write a foreword for this publication. This has been a project which contributes towards one of the aims of the BMHC, that of promoting

1. The Changing Global Religious (Pew Research Centre, April 2017).

better understanding between Muslims and non-Muslim communities.

I hope this publication will benefit all people, young and old, Muslims and non-Muslims from diverse backgrounds and faiths. I request the readers not to judge Islam by the action of some Muslims, but to judge Islam by the actual teachings of Islam.

This book would not have been possible if it was not for the commitment and contribution of the many people who played a part in this project, too many to mention. May God bless them all. If anyone has any suggestions or feedback, please do not hesitate to let us know.

Finally, we also wish to clarify that the contents of this publication do not supersede the laws of the country in which one resides, as it is a prerequisite in Islam for a Muslim to obey the laws of the land.

Nasar Mahmood OBE
Chairman
British Muslim Heritage Centre

An Introductory
Outline

The Prophet Muhammed, (peace and blessings be upon him), according to Islamic tradition, was born in the year 570 (CE). From an early age, Prophet Muhammed (peace and blessings be upon him) came to be known by his people as Al-Sadiq (the Truthful) and Al-Ameen (the Trustworthy) due to his personal integrity. According to Islamic tradition, it was at the age of forty that he received the initial Revelation from God through the Archangel Gabriel. The first person to believe in him as the Messenger of God was his wife, Khadijah.

Prophet Muhammed (peace and blessings be upon him) conveyed the message from God; a message known as "Islam", calling for devotion and submission to God alone. Islam called on people to cast aside the polytheistic religion of their forefathers, and to embrace pure monotheism.

The early followers of Islam suffered considerable persecution by the Makkan tribe of Quraish, as did the followers of prophets and messengers before him. The Quraish vehemently opposed the message of Islam, especially Islam's rejection of idol worship. In the year 622, the Quraish conspired to have the Prophet assassinated but with divine help Muhammed (peace and blessings be upon him) was able to escape from his would-be killers. In the company of Abu Bakr (his closest friend and companion), he reached the city of Yathrib (later renamed Madinah in his honour), and this migration to Madinah corresponds to the beginning of the Islamic calendar (Hijra), 622 CE being the first year of the Hijri calendar.

Questions & Answers

The Concept of God In Islam

1. Who is Allah?
Do Muslims worship a different God?

Some people believe that Muslims worship a God different from the one worshipped by Christians and Jews. This misconception might be due to the fact that Muslims often refer to God as "Allah". Allah is simply the Arabic word for the one true God, who created the universe and all of humanity. Arabic speaking people of all religions refer to God as "Allah". For example, if you pick up an Arabic translation of the Christian Bible you will see the word "Allah" where "God" is used in English. Therefore, Allah is not the God of only the Muslims, but the same God worshipped by all monotheistic faiths. This idea that "Allah" is different from "God" is illogical since it is tantamount to saying the French worship a different "god" because they use the word "Dieu", that Spaniards worship a different "god" because they say "Dios" or that Hebrew speakers worship a different "god" because they call Him "Yahweh".

Muslims worship the God of Adam, Noah, Abraham, Moses, David and Jesus (peace and blessings be upon them). However, it is certainly true that Jews, Christians and Muslims all have different concepts of Almighty God. For example, Muslims and Jews alike reject the Christian concept of the Trinity and the Divinity of Jesus (peace and blessings be upon him). This, however, does not mean that each of these three religions worship a different God – because Muslims believe there is only One True God. Judaism, Christianity and Islam all claim to be "Abrahamic Faiths" and all of them are deemed "monotheistic".

Islam calls upon people to return to the one true God and to worship and obey Him alone. Islam teaches that God should be approached without priestly intermediaries. That is because the merciful all-knowing God is completely in control of everything that exists and He can bestow His grace and mercy upon His creation as He pleases; therefore no intercession, or atonement, is necessary.

It should be clearly understood that Islam is primarily concerned with correcting mankind's concept of Almighty God and not whether we choose to call him Allah or God.

2. The Qur'an says that God is merciful and that He gives severe punishment. So is He forgiving or is He vengeful?

God is just, and His justice necessitates that He rewards those who obey and serve Him, and He also holds to account those who disobey and transgress the divine laws of God. If God did not punish the sinful, wicked and evil people who deserve to be punished, it would not be just. When punishment for wrongdoing is certain, it serves to deter potential offenders. In contrast, if God forgave everyone and

14

punished no one there would be no reason for legislation, ethics or even morality. Life on earth would be chaotic and nothing short of anarchy. However, whilst justice cannot always be obtained on this earth, the Justice of God will be true justice. This justice with its true rewards and just penalties, can only be found with God, and that is what He has promised in the Qur'an:[2]

We will set up scales of justice for the Day of Resurrection so that no one can be wronged in the least, and if there should be even the weight of a mustard seed, We shall bring it out- We take excellent account. [Qur'an, 21: 47][3]

Prophet Muhammed (peace and blessings be upon him) said that God the Almighty said:

"My Mercy prevails over My wrath."[4]

God forgives all those who repent and correct themselves at any stage in their lives, and He has invited all people to His abundant forgiveness and mercy:

Say: "O My slaves who have transgressed against their souls! Despair not of the mercy of Allah. Indeed, Allah forgives all sins. Indeed, it is He who is the Forgiving, the Merciful. And return [in repentance] to your Lord and submit to Him before the punishment comes upon you; then you will not

2. The Qur'an is the word of God, whereas Hadiths are the tradition of the Prophet Muhammed (peace and blessings be upon him).
3. These numbers denote the chapter and verse numbers of the text in the Qur'an.
4. Sahih al-Bukhari, 3022; Sahih Muslim, 2751

be helped. And follow the best of what was revealed
to you from your Lord before the punishment comes
upon you suddenly, while you do not perceive."
[Qur'an, 39: 53–5]

3. Some believe that Muslims worship Muhammed (peace and blessings be upon him). Is this true?

Some people mistakenly assume that Muslims worship
Prophet Muhammed (peace and blessings be upon him).
Muslims do not worship Prophet Muhammed (peace and
blessings be upon him) in any way. Muslims believe that
Prophet Muhammed (peace and blessings be upon him)
was the last messenger sent to earth by God, and like all
other Prophets, such as Moses, Abraham and Jesus, he was
a human being.

Prophet Muhammed (peace and blessings be upon him)
never claimed divine status. He called people to worship
Almighty God alone and he continually insisted he was
nothing more than a human being. In order to prevent his
Deification, Prophet Muhammed (peace and blessings be
upon him) always said he should be referred to as "Allah's
slave and messenger".

Muslims strive to follow the example of Prophet Muhammed
(peace and blessings be upon him) but do not worship him
in any way. Islam teaches Muslims to believe, love and
respect all of God's Prophets and Messengers (peace and
blessings be upon them). However, respecting and loving
them does not mean worshipping them. Muslims firmly
believe that all worship and prayer must only be directed

to the one true God.

In fact, it is considered an unpardonable sin in Islam to worship the Prophet Muhammed (peace and blessings be upon him) – or anyone else – along with, or instead of, Almighty God. Even if a person claims to be a Muslim but then worships or prays to anything other than God, it invalidates their claim to be a Muslim. Islam makes it clear that Muslims must worship one God alone.

4. Is there life after Death?

The Qur'an teaches that the present life is a trial in preparation for the next realm of perpetual existence. A Day will come when the whole universe will come to an end, and the dead will be resurrected to stand in judgment before God.

On the Day when the earth will be changed into a another earth and the heavens as well, and all will appear before Allah – the One, the Supreme.

[Qur'an, 14: 48]

The Day of Resurrection will be the beginning of another life, one that will be eternal. It is then that every person will be fully rewarded by God for their good deeds and punished for their evil deeds, unless they are forgiven.

The explanation that the Qur'an gives about the necessity of life after death is exactly what the moral consciousness of a human being demands. If there was no life after death, the very belief in God would become meaningless, or even if one believed in Him, it would then be an unjust and indifferent deity, having once created the individual and no longer being concerned with his or her fate. The Qur'an emphatically states that the Day of Judgment will come and that God will decide the fate of each soul.

Any person who has suffered injustice, irrespective of financial or social status, almost certainly wants the perpetrator to be held accountable. Though a large number of perpetrators are punished, some of them get off lightly or are never even brought to justice. They may continue to lead pleasant or even luxurious lives and enjoy a peaceful existence. People may escape justice in this world, but they will be held accountable on the Day of Judgment.

While it is true that a wrongdoer may receive the punishment that he or she deserves in this life, it will remain incomplete. The same is true of someone who has done much good, helped or taught many people, saved lives, suffered to uphold truth, or patiently endured much hardship and injustice. No earthly compensation is adequate for such courage and effort. These types of deeds can only be repaid in full in an eternal life, where every individual affected by this person's actions will testify for or against that person, and where every individual's innermost thoughts and intentions, known only to God, will be exposed and judged justly.

Finally, God is able to create and re-create as He wills. Allah, the Exalted, says:

> **On that Day We shall roll up the heavens like a scroll rolled up for books. Just as We produced the first creation, so shall We reproduce it. That is a promise binding on Us. Indeed We will do it.** [Qur'an, 21: 104]

The Qur'an
& Other Scriptures

5. Is the Qur'an the word of God or was it written by Muhammed (peace and blessings be upon him) or plagiarised from the Bible?

It is interesting to note that no other religious scripture claims to be totally the direct word of God as clearly and as often as the Qur'an does. God says:

> **Will they not think about this Qur'an? If it had been from anyone other than God, they would have found in it many inconsistencies.** [Qur'an, 4: 82]

At the time when the Qur'an was revealed, Arabs recognised that the language of the Qur'an was unique and distinctly different from the language spoken by Prophet Muhammed (peace and blessings be upon him) and his people. This was in spite of the fact that the Arabs of that time were known for their skill in poetry and mastery of the Arabic language. Moreover, Muhammed (peace and blessings be upon him) was known to be illiterate and the Qur'an mentions that Prophet Muhammed (peace and blessings be upon him) could not read or write. If the contrary were true, certainly his contemporaries would have exposed him. Without doubt there were some people who rejected Muhammed's message, just as the message of other Prophets had been rejected by their people in the past; but none denied it for this reason. In His divine wisdom, God chose His final Messenger to be an illiterate man so no one would have the slightest justification to doubt him or accuse him of writing or plagiarising other scriptures.

Muhammed's enemies realised that as much as they tried, they could not outdo or even equal this outstanding masterpiece. Furthermore, the Qur'an recounts some instances where Prophet Muhammed (peace and blessings be upon him) was corrected by Allah because of his unintentional human errors. Had he been the author of the Qur'an he would not have included these rebukes of himself in the Qur'an.

Furthermore, the Qur'an contains scientific knowledge that could not have possibly been known at that time by Muhammed (peace and blessings be upon him) or by any other person for that matter. The renowned French scientist, Dr Maurice Bucaille, states that an "encyclopaedic" knowledge is needed to assess such vast scientific wealth. Bucaille also states that, "whilst the Qur'an contains so much scientific knowledge, it is also impossible for the scientist to find inconsistencies in it, unlike many scientific theories."[5] The following are some scientific phenomena mentioned in Qur'an that are in line with established facts:

1. Embryology and the development of foetuses [Qur'an, 23: 12–14].

2. Natural barriers of temperature, salinity, and density between bodies of water in the sea. [Qur'an, 55: 19–20 and 25: 53].

5. Maurice Bucaille, The Bible, The Qur'an and Science, tr. from French by A.D. Pannell & the author, 7th edition (revised), (Paris: Seghers, 1993).

3. Gender differences in plants [Qur'an, 37: 36].

4. An explanation for the Big Bang and the creation of the universe [Qur'an, 21: 31–3].

5. The expansion of the universe [Qur'an, 51: 47 and 21: 30].

6. Ants communicating with each other [Qur'an, 27: 18].

7. Weather cycles [Qur'an, 30: 48, 24: 43 and 23: 12].

8. Bees communicating with each other [Qur'an, 16: 68–9].

9. That mountains have roots, like stakes or pegs [Qur'an, 27: 88 and 78: 6–7].

10. That prior to the creation of the universe there was nothing but dark matter (smoke) [Qur'an, 41: 11].

More and more scientific discoveries are being brought to light which confirm what is stated in the Qur'an. Indeed, some of these scientific discoveries could only have been made thanks to recently discovered facts or newly-invented instruments such as microscopes, telescopes, etc., which did not exist more than 1,400 years ago.

According to Dr Bucaille:

> What initially strikes the reader confronted for the first time with a text of this kind is the sheer abundance of subjects discussed: the Creation, astronomy, the explanation of certain matters concerning the earth, and the animal and vegetable kingdoms, human reproduction. [...] I had to stop and ask myself: if a man was the author of the Qur'an, how could he have written facts in the Seventh century [CE] that today are shown to be in keeping with modern scientific

knowledge?[6]

It is true that there are some similarities between the Qur'an and the Bible, but this is not sufficient to accuse Muhammed (peace and blessings be upon him) of compiling or copying the Bible. The similarities between the two do not indicate that later Prophets plagiarised from previous ones, but merely point to a common source: the One True God, and to the continuation of the same basic message of monotheism.

6. How does the Qur'an differ from other scriptures?

It is an article of faith for every Muslim to believe in all of the prophets and messengers of God and all unadulterated revelations of God. Some of these scriptures still exist today, but as a result of human interference they are not in their pristine form. The Qur'an is the only divine scripture that has stood the test of time. The contents of the Qur'an are exactly the same – to the last word – as it was over 1,400 years ago at the time of the Prophet Muhammed (peace and blessings be upon him). This can be verified from early copies of the Qur'an available in libraries and museums around the world. Not even those who proactively opposed Islam reported any substantiated claims of that nature.

The entire Qur'an was written down during the lifetime of Muhammed (peace and blessings be upon him) by his Companions. In addition, many of the Prophet's Companions memorised the Qur'an as it was being revealed. The Qur'an is still memorised and read in its original Arabic text, and continues to be taught and recited

6. Bucaille, The Bible, The Quran; op cit.

by millions of people around the world.

The Qur'an presents all the prophets of God as belonging to one single brotherhood; all had a similar prophetic mission and conveyed the same basic message, namely, the invitation to worship the same one God; the source of their message was the same. Even if the other Scriptures agree with the Qur'an in the fundamental aspects of the religion, they only address a specific people, and because of this its ruling and regulations are particular to them. It is attributed to Jesus (peace and blessings be upon him) in the Bible that he himself said:

> I was sent only to the lost sheep of the house (Children)
> of Israel. [Matthew, 15: 24]

On the other hand, the Qur'an was revealed to the whole of humanity and not just a specific nation. God says:

> **And We have not sent you [O Muhammed] except to all of mankind, as a Giver of glad tidings and Warner, but most people know not.** [Quran, 34: 28]

Jesus,
The Messenger of God (peace and blessings be upon him)

7. Is it true that Muslims do not believe in Jesus or other Prophets (peace and blessings be upon them)?

A Muslim cannot be a Muslim if he or she does not believe in Jesus (peace and blessings be upon him) as a Prophet of God. Muslims believe in Jesus and in all of God's Prophets (peace and blessings be upon them all). Muslims respect and revere Jesus (peace and blessings be upon him) and await his second coming. According to the Qur'an, he was not crucified but was raised unto Heaven. Muslims consider Jesus (peace and blessings be upon him) among the prominent Messengers of God – but not God or the son of God. Jesus' mother, Mary (peace and blessings be upon her), is regarded as one of the most virtuous and noble women in history, and the Qur'an tells us that Jesus (peace and blessings be upon him) was born miraculously, without a father:

> **Indeed, the example of Jesus in the sight of Allah is like that of Adam. He created him from dust, then said to him, "Be!" And he was!** [Qur'an, 3: 59]

The Qur'an stresses emphatically that God does not have a

"son". Islam teaches that titles such as "Lord" and "Saviour" are for God alone.

8. What does the Qur'an say about Jesus and Mary (peace and blessings be upon them)?

Jesus (peace and blessings be upon him) was among the prominent Messengers who were mentioned in detail in the Qur'an. In fact, there is a chapter in the Qur'an named Maryam (Mary) that speaks about Mary and her son Jesus (peace and blessings be upon them). Jesus (peace and blessings be upon him) is also mentioned in various other chapters throughout the Qur'an. Here is one such quotation:

> **And relate in the Book [the story of] Mary, when she withdrew in seclusion from her family to a place facing east. She took in seclusion from them a screen. Then We sent to her Our angel, and he appeared before her as a man in all respects. She said, "Indeed, I seek refuge in the Most Merciful [God] from you, if you should fear Him." He said, "I am only the messenger of your Lord, to [announce to] you the gift of a pure son." She said; "How can I have a son when no man has touched me, nor am I unchaste?" He said: "Thus [it will be]. Your Lord says, 'It is easy for Me, and We will make him a sign to mankind and a mercy from Us. And it is a matter [already] decreed.'" [Qur'an, 19: 16–21]**

Science & Knowledge

9. What does Islam say about knowledge and science?

Islam encourages the pursuit of knowledge. Worldly knowledge is necessary, and Muslims are encouraged to acquire it in order to benefit themselves and their fellow human beings.

Historically, Muslims have made important contributions in the fields of medicine, mathematics, physics, astronomy, geography, architecture, art, literature, and history, to mention but a few. Algebra, Arabic numerals, trigonometry, etc., were all vital to the advancement of mathematics and science in general. The knowledge of these and other subjects: astronomy, chemistry, optics, etc., were transmitted to Europe from Muslim countries, mainly Muslim Spain in the twelfth century. This occurred when European scholars translated countless scientific works from Arabic into Latin, which contributed to the rise of modern learning and universities in Europe. It was also the Muslims who developed sophisticated instruments, including the astrolabe, the quadrant and good navigational maps, which were to make possible the European voyages of discovery to the New World.

As Wallbank and Schrier stated:

> In medicine, mathematics, astronomy, chemistry and physics, Muslim achievements were particularly noteworthy. Well-equipped hospitals, usually associated with medical schools, were located in the principal cities. At a time when superstition still hampered the practice of medicine in western countries, Muslim physicians were diagnosing diseases, prescribing cures and performing advanced surgery. [...] Probably the greatest of all physicians was the 9th century figure, Al-Razi, known in the West as Rhazes. He was the author of scores of scientific works, including a comprehensive medical encyclopaedia and a pioneering handbook on smallpox and measles. A 10th century physician, Avicenna (Ibn Sina) compiled a huge Cannon of Medicine which was considered the standard guide in European medical circles until the late 17th century. [...] Important advances were made in algebra, analytical geometry and plane spherical trigonometry.[7]

---

7. T. Walter Wallbank and Arnold Schrier, Living World History (Glenview, IL: Scott, Foresman and Co., 1990).

Health

10. Why is the consumption of alcohol prohibited in Islam?

In Islam all things that are harmful or whose harm exceeds their benefit are unlawful. Therefore, alcohol is deemed unlawful in Islam.

Alcohol continues to cost countless human lives and causes misery to millions throughout the world. Statistics showing soaring crime rates, mental illnesses, traffic-related accidents, high incidences of domestic violence, and many millions of broken homes bear witness to the destructive effects of alcohol. Millions of people also die every year as a result of alcohol-related diseases, which include cirrhosis of the liver, high blood pressure, various forms of cancer, pancreatitis and depression. Drinking alcohol also weakens the immune system, making the body vulnerable to infectious diseases, such as pneumonia and tuberculosis. During pregnancy, alcohol consumption also has detrimental harmful effects on the foetus.

In fact, according to a report released by the World Health Organization in 2018, 237 million men and 46 million women annually suffer from alcohol-related disorders.[8] In 2014-2016 in England and Wales, alcohol-related violent incidents

---

8. World Health Organization (WHO), Global Status Report on Alcohol and Health, (2018).

made up 67% of violent incidents which take place at the weekend and 68% of those take place during the evening and night.[9]

God, in His infinite wisdom, made an injunction aimed at preserving the individual and society. Hence the consumption of alcohol is prohibited in Islam. It is worth mentioning that when Muslims refrain from something that God with His absolute wisdom and knowledge has forbidden, they do so because God prohibits what is harmful to His creation in one way or another, to a greater or lesser degree, as is mentioned in the following verse of the Qur'an:

Say (O Prophet): "My Lord only forbids disgraceful deeds whether they be open or hidden." [Qur'an, 7: 33]

9. Office for National Statistics, Overview of Violent Crime and Sexual Offences, (2017).

The Environment & Animal Rights

11. What does Islam say about the environment and animal rights?

Muslims are enjoined to protect their natural surroundings, where they are trusted to manage and preserve the creations of God in a responsible manner:

> **Eat and drink but waste not by extravagance, certainly He (Allah) likes not those who waste by extravagance.** [Qur'an, 7: 31]

Therefore, any resources are to be handled and used with great care, and all forms of waste are to be avoided. This was remarked upon by the modern scholar, Hodgson, who epitomised the exemplary dictates of Islamic consciousness as, "the demand for personal responsibility for the moral ordering of the natural world."[10] Great emphasis is placed upon conservation of water. The Prophet Muhammed (peace and blessings be upon him) stated:

> "Do not waste water even if you are at a running stream."[11]

---

10. Marshall G. Hodgson, The Venture of Islam, vol. 2 (Chicago: University of Chicago Press, 1977).
11. Ahmed, 6768; Ibn Majah, 419.

Benevolence is commended by Prophet Muhammed (peace and blessings be upon him) as the first of all virtues, and it also extends to animals. It is prohibited in Islam to slaughter a she-animal whilst she is feeding her new-born, and no distress is to be inflicted on animals under any circumstance. Cruelty to animals, or killing animals for sport or any other purpose other than for food are forbidden in Islam.

The Prophet (peace and blessings be upon him) advised Muslims about showing kindness towards animals and cautioned believers. It is reported that the Prophet (peace and blessings be upon him) said:

> "Allah had once forgiven a prostitute. She passed by a dog panting near a well. Seeing that thirst had nearly killed him, she took off her shoe, tied it to her scarf, and drew up some water. Allah forgave her for that."[12]

It is also related that the Messenger of God (peace and blessings be upon him) said:

> "A woman was punished due to a cat she had imprisoned until it died, as a result she entered the Hellfire. She did not give the cat any food or water while it was imprisoned, neither did she set it free so it could eat from the vermin of the earth."[13]

12. Sahih al-Bukhari, 3143; Sahih Muslim, 2245
13. Sahih al-Bukhari, 3318

Women
In Islam

12. Does Islam oppress women?

In answering this question, we must differentiate between the teachings of Islam and the practice of some Muslims. Although some Muslim cultures oppress women, it often reflects local customs that are contrary to Islamic teachings. Islam expects its adherents to uphold the rights of women in order to protect their social status and prevent their degradation in any way. Islam further holds that women are equal to men in their honour and their accountability before God.

The idea that Islam treats women as second-class citizens is a myth. Islam elevated the status of women over 1,400 years ago by declaring them the sisters of men, giving them the right to be educated, the right to choose or reject a future husband, the right to end an unhappy marriage, the right to inheritance, and the rights of a full citizen of the state. Not only material and physical rights, but those of kindness and consideration are equally specified and significant.

Men and women are two equally important components of society, and the rights and responsibilities of both genders are equitable and balanced. Roles of men and women are complementary and collaborative. Although their obligations might differ in certain areas of life in accordance with their physical and psychological differences, each is equally accountable for their particular responsibilities.

Under Islamic Jurisprudence, when a Muslim woman marries, she is recommended to keep her maiden name as it is part of her distinct identity and family name.

The Qur'an places the responsibility on men to protect and maintain their female relatives. This also means that a man must provide for his family including his wife, even if she has wealth of her own. She is not obliged to spend any of her money towards the maintenance of her family, though she can do that willingly if she wants to. This relieves a woman of the need to earn a living, but she can work if she chooses to do so, as long as it doesn't adversely affect her family's wellbeing.

The family, like any other organisation, needs order and leadership. The Qur'an states that the husband has a "degree" of authority over his wife, which means guardianship.

13. Under Islamic law, why is a woman's share of inherited wealth half that of a man's?

Islam abolished the former practice of inheritance being distributed to the oldest son or the sons only. According to the Qur'an, a woman automatically inherits from her father, her husband, her son and her childless brother. The Qur'an contains specific guidance regarding the distribution of the inherited wealth among the rightful beneficiaries.

In some cases, the female inherits a share that is half that of the male. However, this is not always so. There are certain instances when they inherit equal shares and, in some cases, a female can inherit a share that is more than that of the male. But even when the male is given a larger share there is a good reason behind it. In Islam, a woman has no financial obligations towards her family, even if she is wealthy or has her own source of income; the financial responsibility always lies upon the man. As long as a woman remains unmarried, it is the legal obligation of her father, brother or other guardian to provide her food, clothing, medication, housing and other financial needs. After she is married, it is the duty of her husband. Islam holds the man financially responsible for fulfilling all the needs of his family.

The difference in shares does not mean that one gender is preferred over the other. It represents a just balance between the roles and responsibilities of family members according to their natural, physical and emotional makeup. Despite this, she receives a share of inheritance, which becomes her own property to save or use as she pleases. No other person has the right to claim any portion of her share. In contrast, the man's share becomes a part of his property from which he is obligated to maintain his family and other female members of the household, so it is constantly being consumed.

Suppose someone died leaving a son and a daughter. The son's share of inheritance may well be depleted when he gives a dowry to his wife and supports his family, including his sister until she marries. Any additional income will have to be earned through his work. However, his sister's share remains untouched, or might even increase if she invests it. When she marries, she will receive a dowry from her husband and will be maintained by him, having no financial responsibilities whatsoever. Thus, some may conclude that Islam has actually favoured women over men.

14. Why do Muslim women wear Hijab?

The matter of women's dress might seem trivial to some, especially in today's modern societies; however, Islam assigns social and legal dimensions to its morals. When men and women observe the proper Islamic dress, they not only protect their own honour and reputation, but they contribute greatly towards peace and order in society.

Men and women are expected to be chaste, modest and avoid any type of dress and conduct that may invite temptation. Both are instructed to guard their chastity. God directs men first and then women in the Qur'an:

> **Tell believing men to lower their glances and guard their private parts: that is purer for them. God is well aware of everything they do. And tell believing women that they should lower their glances, guard their private parts, and not display their charms beyond what [it is acceptable] to reveal; they should let their headscarves fall to cover their necklines and not reveal their charms except to their husbands, their fathers, their husbands' fathers, their sons, their husbands' sons, their brothers, their brothers' sons, their sisters' sons. [Qur'an, 24: 30–1]**

15. Why does Islam permit polygamy?

Polygamy is a form of marriage wherein a person has more than one spouse. Polygamy can be of two types. The first type is called polygyny, where a man marries more than one woman, and the other is polyandry, where a woman marries more than one man. In Islam, a limited form of polygyny is permitted, whereas polyandry is prohibited.

In contrast to Islam, one will not find a limit for the number of wives in the Jewish Talmud or the Christian Bible. According to these scriptures, there is no limit to how many women a man may marry. Therefore, polygyny is not something exclusive to Islam. In the early teachings of Christianity, men were permitted to take as many wives as they wished, since the Bible placed no limit on the number of wives a man could marry. It was only in recent centuries that the Catholic Church limited the number of wives to one.

At a time when men were permitted to an unlimited number of wives, Islam capped the number to a maximum of four. Islam gives men permission to marry up to four women, on the condition that he deals with all of them equitably and justly, as indicated by God's statement:

> **But if you fear that you will not be just, then marry only one.** [Quran [4: 3]

It is not incumbent upon Muslims to practice polygamy. In Islam, taking an additional wife is neither encouraged nor prohibited.

John Esposito, a professor of religion and international

affairs and Islamic studies at Georgetown University, writes: "Although it is found in many religious and cultural traditions, polygamy is most often identified with Islam in the minds of Westerners. In fact, the Qur'an and Islamic Law sought to control and regulate the number of spouses rather than give free license." He continues:

> The Qur'an allows a man to marry up to four wives, provided he can support and treat them all equally. Muslims regard this Quranic command as strengthening the status of women and the family for it sought to ensure the welfare of single women and widows in a society whose male population was diminished by warfare, and to curb unrestricted polygamy.[14]

There are certain circumstances which warrant the taking of another wife. For example, if there is a surplus of unmarried women in society, especially during times of war when mortality rates among males are higher than females and widows are in need of shelter and care. The average life span of females is also generally longer than that of males, and statistically, more men die due to accidents and diseases than women. As a result, at any given time there may be a shortage of men in comparison to women. Therefore, even if every single man married one woman, there would still be millions of women who would not be able to find a husband.

In modern society, it is not uncommon for a married man to have extramarital affairs. Seldom is this practice scorned, despite the harms that stem from it. It is also well known that

14. John Esposito, Islam: The Straight Path (Oxford: Oxford University Press, 1988).

the majority of men who visit prostitutes are married men. All of which can result in serious consequences of marital and social breakdowns, and even health problems.

There is no doubt that a second wife who is lawfully married and treated with honour is better off than a mistress without any legal rights or social respect. Islam prohibits fornication and adultery, and only permits polygamy under strict conditions.

16. If a man is permitted to have more than one wife, then why can't a woman have more than one husband?

Islam teaches that God has created men and women as equal in their rights and intellect but not as identical beings. They are different physically and psychologically and each has different capabilities. Their roles and responsibilities are therefore different but they complement one another.

Some may object to a man having the right to more than one wife by insisting that, in fairness, women should also be able to practice polyandry. However, the following few points could be part of the reason behind its prohibition by God:

- One of the benefits of polygyny is that it solves the problem of women outnumbering men; i.e. in societies such as in China, America and various other countries where women outnumber men by millions.

- Islam assigns great importance to the recognition of

parents, both the mother and father. When a man has more than one wife, the parents of two children born in such marriages can easily be identified. But in the case of a woman with more than one husband, without resorting to sophisticated laboratory tests, only the mother of the child born would be known but not the father.

17. Why does Islam impose such harsh punishments for sex outside marriage?

Islam views adultery as a serious wrongdoing because it undermines the very foundation of the family system upon which the whole structure of society is built. Illicit relationships destabilise the family and eventually bring about the breakdown of the system.

Nowadays, some are opposed to the Islamic punishment for fornication and adultery because they see it as disproportionate or too harsh a punishment for the crime. The basic problem here is the different standards by which the severity of the crime is measured.

Punishment in Islam has a social purpose, which is to dissuade transgressors from harming others and society. The nature of the punishment depends on the seriousness of the unlawful act in question.

- Only a legitimate government has the right to pass judgments and penalise those who transgress the rules regarding adultery.

- Any case that comes before the court for judgment

must be investigated thoroughly and proper evidence must be brought before the court to satisfy all the requirements of Islamic law. Conviction is subject to a high standard of proof. The evidence must be a "confession" or "four eyewitnesses" or the pregnancy of an unmarried woman – if evidence is missing the conviction cannot be upheld. The result is that the punishment is rarely carried out and serves primarily as a deterrent.

Islam, Jihad
& Terrorism

18. What is Shariah Law?

Shariah is the Islamic Law – the disciplines and principles that govern the various aspects of public and private life, including the behaviour of an individual Muslim towards themselves, family, neighbours, community, city, nation, the environment and society as a whole. Similarly, Shariah governs the interactions between communities, groups and social and economic organisations. Shariah establishes the norms by which all social actions are classified, categorised and administered within the overall governance of the state. Shariah is comprised of five main branches: morals and manners, ritual worship, beliefs, transactions and contracts, and penal code. Therefore, Shariah law is in fact Islam's entire legal system and not just a set of punishments, as it is often incorrectly, wrongly stated and assumed.

Some parts of Shariah can be described as "law" in the usual sense of that word, while other parts are better understood as rules for living life in accordance with God's will. Arab Christians and Arab Jews use the same word, "Shariah", to describe their own religious laws.

19. Is Islam a violent religion?

Islam considers all life as sacred, but in particular emphasises the sanctity of human life. God says in the Qur'an:

> **Whoever takes a life — unless as a punishment for murder or mischief in the land — it will be as if they killed all of humanity; and whoever saves a life, it will be as if they saved all of humanity.** [Qur'an, 5: 32]

Even in a state of war, Islam enjoins that armies deal with the enemy justly in the battlefield. Islam has drawn a clear line of distinction between the combatants and the non-combatants. The Prophet (peace and blessings be upon him) ordered his armies:

> "Do not kill any old person, any child or any woman."[15]

And he said:

> "Do not kill the monks in monasteries."[16]

Once, upon seeing the corpse of a woman on a battlefield, the Prophet Muhammed (peace and blessings be upon him) angrily asked his companions why she had been killed, and he strongly condemned the atrocious act. For those enemies active in combat and those taken as prisoners of war, the list of rights is lengthy. There should be no torture; no killing of the wounded or defenseless; no mutilation of enemy bodies, and; return of corpses to the enemy must be honoured.

---

15. Abu Dawud: 2614
16. Al-Bayhaqi, Sunan al-Kubra.

Far from being a militant dogma, Islam is a way of life that transcends race and ethnicity. The Qur'an repeatedly reminds us of our common origin:

> **O mankind, indeed we created you from a male and a female, and made you peoples and tribes that you may know one another. Verily the most noble amongst you in the sight of Allah is the most righteous of you.** [Qur'an, 49: 13]

20. What is "Jihad"?

While Islam is generally misunderstood in the West, perhaps no other Islamic term evokes such strong reaction as Jihad. The Arabic word, "Jihad", which is almost always mistranslated as "holy war", simply means "to struggle" or "to exert one's utmost effort". It is incorrect to imagine that jihad is synonymous only with fighting or war, for this is but one particular aspect of the term. Jihad is a struggle to do good and to remove injustice, oppression and evil from oneself and from society. This struggle is spiritual, social, economic and political.

Indeed, the concept of jihad is part of life, and it has multiple dimensions not limited only to armed struggle. For example, one finds in the Qur'an mention of "jihad by means of the Qur'an", which means an invitation to the truth with evidence, clarifying and presenting the best argument. There is also "Jihad of the Soul", which means striving to purify the soul, to increase one's faith and incline it towards good while keeping away from wrongdoing. Then there is "jihad through wealth", which means spending in a way so that it benefits others, such as charity and welfare. And there is "jihad through the self", which comprises all good work done by a believer, such as teaching, disseminating knowledge and finally, lawful armed struggle, i.e. self-defense against aggression.

Invite to the way of your Lord with wisdom and good instruction, and argue with them in a way that is best. [Qur'an, 16: 125]

In the name of jihad, Islam calls for social reform and the elimination of ignorance, superstition, poverty, disease and racial discrimination. Among its main goals is the protection of rights for the weaker members of society against the excesses and injustices of the powerful and influential. Islam prohibits injustice. God, the Exalted, says in the Qur'an:

And do not let the hatred of a people prevent you from being just. Be just; that is nearer to righteousness. [Qur'an, 5: 8]

Enmity toward any people or nation should not provoke Muslims to commit aggression against them, oppress them or disregard their rights.

As Prophet Muhammed (peace and blessings be upon him) said: "One of the highest levels of jihad is to stand up to a tyrant and speak the truth." Restraining oneself from wrongdoing is also a great form of jihad. Another form of jihad is to take up arms in defense of one's country, if attacked. It needs to be made clear that Islam acknowledges war only when all peaceful means such as dialogue, negotiations, and treaties have failed, and only then it becomes the last option for solving problems such as oppression and aggression and for the defence of certain freedoms and rights which can be perceived by any person of reason and logic.

The purpose of jihad is therefore not to convert people by force, or to colonise their country, or to acquire land or wealth, or for self-glorification. Its purpose is basically the protection of life, property, land, honour and freedom for oneself as well as protection of others from injustice and oppression.

21. Are Muslims terrorists?

Unfortunately, nowadays for some, Islam has become synonymous with "terrorism". Far from promoting terrorism, Islam teaches its followers to maintain and promote peace and justice throughout the world. Islam does not condone "terrorism" as defined and understood at present, such as hijacking planes, hostage taking and the torture and killing of innocents in order to achieve political or even religious goals.

The question that poses itself is: Do the teachings of Islam encourage terrorism? Certainly not – Islam entirely prohibits all terrorist acts. It should be remembered that all religions have misguided followers who use their religion as an excuse to achieve certain goals in politics or otherwise. To be even-handed and just, one must consider the actual teachings of the religion, as they are the yardstick by which the actions of its followers can be assessed as being right or wrong.

It is unfair to judge Islam by the wrongdoings of some

deviant Muslims. In fact, what Islam preaches is one thing and what some followers may practice is something completely different. The only way we can do justice to Islam is to find out about its teachings, which are clearly set out in the Qur'an and Prophetic traditions. Former pop singer Cat Stevens, now known as Yusuf Islam, observed: "It is wrong to judge Islam in the light of the behaviour of some deviant Muslims who are always shown on the media. It is like judging a car as unfit if the driver is drunk and he crashes it into a wall."

Islam is a religion of peace, which is practised by submitting one's will to the will of the supreme Creator, God. Islam promotes peace but at the same time it exhorts its followers to work for justice.

Certainly, Islam allows war under particular circumstances, such as self-defense, but Islam never condones attacks against innocent people, women or children. Islam also clearly forbids "taking the law into one's own hands", which means that individual Muslims cannot go around deciding who they want to punish. Trial and punishment must only be carried out by lawful authorities of the state in which one resides.

22. How can Islam be called a "religion of peace" when it was "spread by the sword"?

It is another common misconception among some non-Muslims that Islam would not have gained over 1.8 billion followers all over the world if it were not for the use of force. The following makes it clear that far from being forcefully "spread by the sword", it was the inherent force of truth and its moral and natural appeal that was responsible for the rapid popularity of Islam.

Islam has always given respect and freedom of religion to all faiths. Freedom of religion is ordained in the Qur'an itself:

Let there be no compulsion in religion, for the truth stands out clearly from falsehood. [Qur'an, 2: 256]

The noted historian De Lacy O'Leary wrote: "History makes it clear however, that the legend of fanatical Muslims sweeping through the world and forcing Islam at the point of the sword upon conquered races is one of the most fantastically absurd myths that historians have repeated."[17] The Qur'an says in this connection:

Invite to the way of your Lord with wisdom and good instruction and argue with them in a way that is best. [Qur'an, 16: 125]

Further facts that prove the peaceful nature of Islam:

- Indonesia has the world's largest Muslim population and the majority of the population in Malaysia are Muslims too. On no occasion in history has a Muslim army ever invaded Indonesia or Malaysia; it is well established that Islam became popular in Indonesia due to its moral message. The impact of the faith in particular was to ban immoral and wicked practices, such as female sacrifice, cannibalism, gambling, drug use, the slave trade and alcohol use, which all

17. De Lacy O'Leary, Islam at the Crossroads (London: Kegan Paul, Trench, Trubner & Co., 1923).

prevailed on a general scale prior to the arrival of Islam.

• Muslims ruled Spain (Andalusia) for about 800 years. During this period, Christians and Jews enjoyed freedom to practise their respective religions, free from any constraints. The Jews in fact retained their freedom, privileges, and high status until the end of Muslim rule on the Peninsula and only fled after the start of the Spanish Inquisition.

• Muslims ruled India for about a thousand years, and therefore had the power to force each and every non-Muslim resident of India to convert to Islam, but they did not. Thus 80 per cent of the population of India remains non-Muslim.

• Similarly, Islam is popular in Sub-Saharan Africa and likewise, no Muslim army was ever dispatched there.

In his book The World's Religions, Huston Smith discusses how Prophet Muhammed (peace and blessings be upon him) granted freedom of religion to the Jews and Christians under Muslim rule: "The Prophet had a document drawn up in which he stipulated that Jews and Christians 'shall be protected from all insults and harm; they shall have an equal right with our own people to our assistance and good office', and further, 'they shall practice their religion as freely as the Muslims.'"[18]

Smith points out that Muslims regard the document as the first charter of freedom of conscience in human history and

---

18. Huston Smith, The World's Religions: Our Great Wisdom Traditions (San Francisco: Harper, 1991).

the authoritative model for every subsequent Muslim state.

23. Does the Qur'an say that Muslims should kill non-believers wherever they find them?

There are a few verses from the Qur'an that are quoted out of context to perpetuate the myth that Islam promotes violence and exhorts its followers to kill those outside the fold of Islam. The phrase "kill the polytheists wherever you find them" is often quoted to portray that Islam promotes violence, bloodshed and brutality.

In order to gain context, it is necessary to read from the beginning of the chapter. It discloses that there was a peace treaty between the Muslims and the pagans of Makkah. The pagans violated this treaty by conspiring and facilitating the killing of Muslims, so a period of four months was given to them to make amends; otherwise war would be declared against them. The whole verse actually says:

> **But once the Sacred Months have passed, kill the polytheists (who violated their treaties) wherever you find them, capture them, besiege them, and lie in wait for them on every way. But if they repent, perform prayers, and pay alms-tax, then set them free. Indeed, Allah is All-Forgiving, Most Merciful.**
> [Qur'an, 9: 5]

This verse is a command to the Muslims who had entered into an agreement with those who had persecuted, tortured and expelled them from their homes in the first place, who then violated the agreement. It would seem that any open-minded person would consider the historical context of this verse and agree that it cannot be used as "evidence" that Islam promotes violence, brutality and bloodshed, or that it exhorts its followers to kill anyone outside the fold of Islam.

The very next verse gives the answer to the allegation that Islam promotes violence, brutality and bloodshed:

If any one of the polytheists asks you for protection, then grant it to him so that he may hear the Words of Allah [i.e. the Qur'an]. Then escort him to a place of safety. That is because they are a people who do not know. [Qur'an, 9: 6]

The Universality
of The Message of Islam

24. Is it true that Islam is a religion only for Arabs?

This is not true. Only about 15 to 20 per cent of Muslims in the world are Arabs. There are more Indian Muslims than Arab Muslims, and more Indonesian Muslims than Indian Muslims. The assumption that Islam is the religion of the Arabs is possibly based on the fact that most of the early converts to Islam were Arabs, that the Qur'an is in Arabic, and that the Prophet Muhammed (peace and blessings be upon him) was an Arab.

History testifies that the Prophet (peace and blessings be upon him) and his followers and the early Muslims made every effort to convey the message of Islam to all nations, races and peoples. From the very beginning of the mission of Prophet Muhammed (peace and blessings be upon him), his followers came from a wide spectrum of countries and races. Among them were Bilal, the Abyssinian slave; Suhaib, the Byzantine Roman; Abdullah bin Salam, the Jewish Rabbi; and Salman, the Persian.

Furthermore, it should be clarified that not all Muslims are Arabs and not all Arabs are Muslims. An Arab might be a Muslim, a Christian or a follower of any other religion/

ideology or none. Additionally, some countries – such as Turkey and Iran – which uninformed people consider to be "Arab" are not Arab at all. The people who live in those countries speak languages other than Arabic and are of a different ethnic heritage.

Since truth is eternal and unchanging, and humanity is considered one universal brotherhood, Islam is a message for all people regardless of race, nationality, cultural or linguistic background. A brief look at the Muslim World, from Morocco to Bosnia and from India to Malaysia, is sufficient proof that Islam offers a universal appeal; not to mention the fact that a significant number of Europeans and Americans of all races and ethnic backgrounds are practising Islam. The Qur'an clearly says:

> **And we have not sent you [O Muhammed] except as a Giver of glad tidings and a Warner to all mankind, but most men know not.** [Qur'an, 34: 28]

25. All religions basically teach their followers to do good, so why should a person follow Islam?

In the Qur'an, God says:

(i) **This day, I have perfected for you your religion, completed my favour upon you, and have chosen for you Islam as your religion.** [Qur'an, 5: 3]

(ii) **True Religion, in God's eyes, is Islam: [devotion to Him alone].** [Qur'an, 3: 19]

Islamic Beliefs

The Islamic creed did not begin with the prophethood of Muhammed (peace and blessings be upon him), nor was it invented by him. It is essentially a continuation of the same message contained in previous divine scriptures and taught by all Prophets of God.

Islamic beliefs are eternal truths that neither change nor evolve; they provide truth about God and His relationship with the visible and invisible aspects of the universe, about the reality of this life, the individual's role therein and what will become of such a person afterwards. The pillars of the Islamic faith are: the belief in one God, in His angels, in His scriptures, in His Prophets including Noah, Abraham, Moses, David and Jesus (peace and blessings be upon them all), through all of whom His revelations were conveyed to humanity. Also, belief in the eternal life after death and in God's perfect judgment and complete authority over human destiny.

I   Belief in God

Muslims believe in one eternal and unique God. He is the Creator of all that exists, yet He cannot be compared to anything of His creation. Muslims acknowledge that God alone is Divine, that He alone is the Creator and Sustainer of creation. He is All-Knowing and All-Powerful, The Just and The Merciful.

God is not part of His own creation, nor is any of it a part of Him. The significance of exclusive divinity is that no one and nothing in existence is worthy to be worshipped and obeyed except God, the Creator and Sustainer of all things. In Islam, everything is built upon the Oneness of God. No act of worship has any meaning if the concept of monotheism is in any way compromised.

II   Belief in the Angels

Muslims believe that Angels exist. They obey God and fulfil His commands. God has revealed to us the names of some of the angels, such as Gabriel who was given the task of bringing revelation from God to the Prophets. There is also the Angel of Death, who has been given the task of collecting the souls of people at their appointed times of death.

III   Belief in the Scriptures

Muslims also believe in the original scriptures revealed by God, such as the Scriptures of Abraham and Moses, the Torah, the Psalms of David, and the Gospel of Jesus (peace and blessings be upon them all). However, the original scriptures are no longer available as they were revealed.[19] The final revelation to humanity is the Qur'an, which was revealed to Prophet Muhammed (peace and blessings be upon him). The Qur'an remains preserved and unchanged in its original Arabic text since the time of revelation, which was fourteen centuries ago. There is only one version of the Qur'an. It is studied, recited and memorised by Muslims

---

19. Bart D. Ehrman, Misquoting Jesus: The Story Behind Who Changed the Bible and Why (New York: HarperOne, 2007).

throughout the world. It is God's final message to humanity. It is legislation which encompasses all spheres of human life and it applies to all people, for all time.

IV   Belief in the Messengers

A Muslim is required to believe that God chose the finest among humanity to be Messengers, whom He sent to His creation with a specific message: to worship and obey Him and to establish His religion and His Oneness. God, the Almighty, says:

And We did not send any Messenger before you [O Muhammed] but We inspired him, [saying]: "None has the right to be worshipped but I (Allah), so worship Me (alone and nothing else)." [Qur'an, 21: 25]

All the Prophets preached the same basic message: the worship of the one God alone. In essence, they all preached Islam, which means wilful, peaceful submission to the one true God, Creator and Sustainer of the universe and all that exists.

Prophet Muhammed (peace and blessings be upon him) exemplified the principles laid down in the Qur'an, and true Muslims strive to follow his example. His biography has been recorded in minute detail and is easily accessible for study. There is a complete, authentically narrated documentation of his sayings and practices. It is complementary to the Qur'an and supplements it with additional details and clarification of meanings.

V   Belief in the Last Day

Muslims believe that the life of this world will come to an end and then all the people of the world, from the first to the last of them, will be resurrected for judgement. God mentions:

Whatsoever is on it (i.e. the earth) will perish.
[Qur'an, 55: 26]

The Day of Resurrection is the day when each individual will stand before God and will be questioned about their deeds. The punishment for those who committed evil, unless they are forgiven by God through His Mercy, is justice, while the reward for those who did good is much greater – comprehensive and complete satisfaction and happiness. People will be judged according to their belief and degree of righteousness and nothing else. God says:

Whoever will come to Allah with a good deed shall have ten times as much, and whoever will come to Allah with an evil deed shall have only the like thereof. [Qur'an, 6: 160]

VI   Belief in Pre-Destination

God's knowledge encompasses everything. There is nothing beyond God's knowledge. God knows everything that has happened and everything that will happen.

The Requirements of
Islam

The five "pillars" of Islam make up the practical framework of a Muslim's life, they are:

1. Sincerely reciting the "Shahadah," the Declaration of Faith

To be a Muslim, one must believe and declare the statement: "There is no deity worthy of worship except Allah and Muhammed (peace and blessings be upon him) is His slave and Messenger." This declaration testifies that God exists, that He is unlike any of His creation, and that none is worthy of worship but Him. It also testifies that He is the Creator and Proprietor of all that exists and Disposer of all affairs. God says in the Qur'an:

> **Certainly to Allah (alone) belong all those in the heavens and all those on the earth. And what do those who associate others with Allah really follow? They follow nothing but assumptions and do nothing but lie.** [Qur'an, 10: 66]

The Shahadah (the declaration of faith) also testifies that Muhammed (peace and blessings be upon him) is among the Prophets who conveyed God's revelation to humankind.

God says:

> **And We have not sent you [O Muhammed] except to all of humankind, as a Giver of glad tidings and a Warner, but most people know not.** [Qur'an, 34: 28]

In fact, it is stated in the Qur'an that Muhammed (peace and blessings be upon him) is the last of God's messengers. God says:

> **Muhammed is not the father of any of your men, but he is the Messenger of God and the last of the Prophets.** [Qur'an, 33: 40]

The Qur'an also confirms that Muhammed's teachings are infallible and conveyed from God. God says:

> **Nor does he speak of (his own) desire. It is no less than inspiration sent down to him.** [Qur'an, 53: 3-4]

Thus the Qur'an and Sunnah (practices and sayings) of the final Prophet are the basis of the religion of Islam, and they define every aspect of every individual's way of life.

2. Performing the "Salah", or Formal Obligatory Prayer

Throughout history, prayer was practised in some form or another by all the Prophets and their followers as an indispensable part of God's religion. Islam, the final message to humanity, considers prayer essential. A Muslim is required to pray five times daily within specified intervals, as an expression of gratitude to God for His blessings, favours and mercy. These prayers are obligatory, and form a direct connection between the worshipper and his Creator.

3. Payment of "Zakah," the Obligatory Annual Charity

An important principle of Islam is that all things belong to God, and Muslims are enjoined to earn and spend their wealth in ways that are acceptable to God. The literal meaning of Zakah is 'to cleanse' or 'purification', and in Islam Zakah means purifying your wealth for the will of God. Zakah is also a spiritual purification which serves as a means to draw an individual closer to God.

A Zakah of 2.5 per cent is payable annually to charity. However, Zakah is only due when a person owns the minimum qualifying amount of wealth or savings which has been kept for a full lunar year.

Zakah cleanses a person of greed, selfishness, base covetousness, and the love of this temporary world. God says:

And whoever is saved from the selfishness of their own souls, it is they who are (truly) successful. [Qur'an, 59: 9]

It is the ideal way to provide for and meet the needs of the poorer sections of society without causing hardship to the wealthy.

4. Fasting, or "Siyam," during the month of Ramadhan

God has enjoined fasting upon the Muslims as He enjoined it upon previous nations. He, the Exalted, says:

You who believe, fasting is prescribed for you, as

it was prescribed for those before you, so that you may be mindful of God. [Qur'an, 2: 183]

Fasting, which involves abstinence from eating, drinking, sexual intercourse and all bad habits such as smoking, is observed throughout the daylight hours of the lunar month of Ramadhan. When done in obedience to God's command, fasting teaches believers patience and self-control, as well as reminding them of their responsibility toward the millions of human beings who lack provisions themselves or are victims of the unjust distribution of wealth. The month of fasting is accompanied by increased efforts toward good manners and righteous deeds, along with additional worship at night. Fasting is not a retreat from life; rather, it is a supplement to a Muslim's ordinary activities.

5. Making the "Hajj", or Pilgrimage, to Makkah

Muslims are obliged to make the once in a lifetime pilgrimage to Makkah if they are physically and financially capable of undertaking the journey, and can support their family during their absence. God says:

Pilgrimage to the House (i.e. the Ka'bah) is a duty people owe to Allah, (upon) everyone who is able to undertake the journey to it. [Qur'an 3: 97]

Millions of Muslims travel to Makkah each year from every corner of the globe, providing a unique opportunity to follow in the footsteps of the previous Prophets such as Abraham, Moses, Muhammad and others (peace and blessings be upon them all). Hajj is an expression of pure faith and total submission to His command, and the pilgrim performs rites of unconditional obedience, seeking nothing but the acceptance of their efforts and forgiveness of their past sins.

Who Is Muhammed?

Muhammed (peace and blessings be upon him) was a man of noble descent and an example of excellent manners. God, the Exalted, praised him saying:

And verily, [O Muhammed] you are on the most exalted (standard of) character. [Qur'an, 68: 4]

Even his enemies attested to his excellent manners. Abu Jahl, who was one of the harshest enemies of Islam, said: "O Muhammed! I do not say that you are a liar!" Some of his Companions described his manners saying:

He was never rough. He never raised his voice in public or used foul language. He did not respond to evil with evil; rather, he forgave and pardoned. He did not raise his hand to hit a servant or woman. He would not become angry if he was wronged, nor would he avenge himself. He only became angry when people transgressed the limits and boundaries of Allah. The Prophet was not given a choice between two matters, except that he chose the easier of the two, as long as it was not a sinful act. If that act was a sinful act, he would be the farthest from it. When he entered his home, he was a normal individual, he would clean his clothes, milk his sheep, and serve himself.[20]

20. Al-Jumuah Staff, Discover Islam (Riyadh: Al-Jumuah Magazine for Editing & Pub., 2003).

In his ground-breaking work, On Heroes, Hero-worship and the Heroic in History, Thomas Carlyle writes the following about Muhammed:

> But, from an early age, he had been remarked as a thoughtful man. His companions named him "Al-Amin, The Faithful." A man of truth and fidelity; true in what he did, in what he spoke and thought. They noted that [when he spoke] he always meant something. A man rather taciturn in speech; silent when there was nothing to be said; but pertinent, wise, sincere, when he did speak; always throwing light on the matter. [...] Through life we find him to have been regarded as an altogether solid, brotherly, genuine man. A serious, sincere character; yet amiable, cordial, companionable, jocose[21] even – a good laugh in him withal; there are men whose laugh is as untrue as anything about them; who cannot laugh. [...] A spontaneous, passionate, yet just, true-meaning man![22]

Prophecies about Muhammed (peace and blessings be upon him)

Prophet Jesus (peace and blessings be upon him) foretold the coming of another Prophet, whose name would be "Periqlytos", or "Paraclete", or "Paracalon" and who (that is, whose teachings) would last forever:

> "I will pray the Father, and He shall give you another Comforter (Periqlytos), that he may abide with you

---

21. Meaning playful or humorous.
22. Thomas Carlyle, 'The Hero as Prophet', in On Heroes, Hero-worship and the Heroic in History, (London: Chapman and Hall, 1840).

forever." [John, 14: 16]

The word periqlytos means 'illustrious, renowned' and 'praiseworthy' and this is exactly what the name 'Ahmad', which was one the names of Prophet Muhammed, means. It is confirmed in the Qur'an that the Prophet Jesus (peace and blessings be upon him) prophesied that a Prophet named 'Ahmad' would come after him. God, the Exalted, says in the Qur'an:

> **And remember when Jesus the son of Mary, said: "O Children of Israel! I am the Messenger of Allah unto you, confirming the Torah which come before me, and giving glad tidings of a Messenger to come after me, whose name shall be Ahmad."** [Qur'an, 61: 6]

What Non-Muslims Say About Muhammed (peace and blessings be upon him)

Annie Besant, (1847–1933) –British socialist, theosophist, women's rights activist, writer, orator, and supporter of both Irish and Indian self-rule:

> It is impossible for anyone who studies the life and character of the great Prophet of Arabia, who knows how he taught and how he lived, to feel anything but reverence for that mighty Prophet, one of the great messengers of the Supreme. And although in what I put to you I shall say many things which may be familiar to many, yet I myself feel whenever I re-read them, a new way of admiration, a new sense of reverence for that mighty Arabian teacher.[23]

23. Annie Besant, The Life and Teachings of Muhammad (Madras: Adyar, 1932).

Sir George Bernard Shaw, (1856–1950) – Irish comic dramatist, literary critic, and socialist propagandist, winner of the Nobel Prize for Literature in 1925:

> I have always held the religion of Muhammad in high estimation because of its wonderful vitality. It is the only religion which appears to me to possess that assimilating capacity to the changing phase of existence which can make itself appeal to every age. I have studied him – the wonderful man and in my opinion far from being an anti-Christ, he must be called the Saviour of Humanity.

> I believe that if a man like him were to assume the dictatorship of the modern world he would succeed in solving its problems in a way that would bring it the much-needed peace and happiness: I have prophesied about the faith of Muhammad that it would be acceptable to the Europe of tomorrow as it is beginning to be acceptable to the Europe of today.[24]

James Michener, (1907–1997) – U.S. novelist and short-story writer:

> No other religion in history spread so rapidly as Islam. The West has widely believed that this surge of religion was made possible by the sword. But no modern scholar accepts this idea, and the Qur'an is explicit in the support of the freedom of conscience.

> Like almost every major prophet before him, Muhammad fought shy of serving as the transmitter

24. Sir George Bernard Shaw, The Genuine Islam, vol. 1, no. 8 (Singapore, 1936).

of God's word sensing his own inadequacy. But the Angel commanded "Read". So far as we know, Muhammad was unable to read or write, but he began to dictate those inspired words which would soon revolutionize a large segment of the earth: "There is one God."

In all things Muhammad was profoundly practical. When his beloved son Ibrahim died, an eclipse occurred and rumours of God's personal condolence quickly arose. Whereupon Muhammad is said to have announced, "An eclipse is a phenomenon of nature. It is foolish to attribute such things to the death or birth of a human being."

At Muhammad's own death an attempt was made to deify him, but the man who was to become his administrative successor killed the hysteria with one of the noblest speeches in religious history: "If there are any among you who worshiped Muhammad, he is dead. But if it is God you Worshiped, He lives forever."[25]

Michael H. Hart (b. 1932) – Professor of astronomy, physics and the history of science:

My choice of Muhammad to lead the list of the world's most influential persons may surprise some readers and may be questioned by others, but he was the only man in history who was supremely successful on both the religious and secular level.[26]

---

25. James A. Michener, 'Islam: The Misunderstood Religion', Reader's Digest (May 1955).
26. Michael H. Hart, The 100: A Ranking of the Most Influential Persons in History (New York: Carol Publishing Group, 1978).

William Montgomery Watt (1909–2006) – Professor (Emeritus) of Arabic and Islamic Studies at the University of Edinburgh:

> His readiness to undergo persecutions for his beliefs, the high moral character of the men who believed in him and looked up to him as leader, and the greatness of his ultimate achievement – all argue his fundamental integrity. To suppose Muhammad an impostor raises more problems than it solves. Moreover, none of the great figures of history is so poorly appreciated in the West as Muhammad.[27]

Alphonse de Lamartine (1790-1869) – French poet and statesman:

> Philosopher, orator, apostle, legislator, warrior, conqueror of ideas, restorer of rational dogmas, of a cult without images; the founder of twenty terrestrial empires and of one spiritual empire, that is Muhammad. As regards all standards by which human greatness may be measured, we may well ask, is there any man greater than he?[28]

Reginald Bosworth Smith (1839–1908) – Late Fellow of Trinity College, Oxford:

> ... he was Caesar and Pope in one; but he was Pope without the Pope's pretensions, and Caesar without the legions of Caesar. Without a standing army,

---

27. William Montgomery Watt, Muhammad at Mecca (Oxford: Oxford University Press, 1953).
28. Translated from Alphonse de Lamartine, Histoire de La Turquie vol. II (Paris: Victor Lecou, 1854).

without a bodyguard, without a palace, without a fixed revenue, if ever any man had the right to say that he ruled by a right Divine, it was Muhammed; for he had all the power without its instruments and without its supports.[29]

Mohandas Karamchand Gandhi (1869–1948) – Indian thinker, statesman, and nationalist leader:

I became more than ever convinced that it was not the sword that won a place for Islam in those days in the scheme of life. It was the rigid simplicity, the utter self-effacement of the prophet, the scrupulous regard for his pledges, his intense devotion to his friends and followers, his intrepidity, his fearlessness, his absolute trust in God and in his own mission. These, and not the sword carried everything before them and surmounted every trouble.[30]

Edward Gibbon (1737–1794) – Considered the greatest British historian of his time:

The greatest success of Mohammad's life was effected by sheer moral force without the stroke of a sword.[31]

His (i.e., Muhammed's) memory was capacious and retentive, his wit easy and social, his imagination sublime, his judgment clear, rapid and decisive. He possessed the courage of both thought and action.[32]

---

29. Reginald Bosworth Smith, Mohammed and Mohammedanism (London: Smith, Elder & Co., 1874).
30. Statement by Gandhi in Young India, Vol. X. (1928).
31. Edward Gibbon, History of the Saracen Empire (London: Alex Murray and Son, 1870).
32. Edward Gibbon, History of the Decline and Fall of the Roman Empire, vol. 5, (London: John Murray, 1838).

John William Draper (1811–1882) – American scientist, philosopher, and historian:

> Four years after the death of Justinian, A.D. 569, was born at Mecca, in Arabia, the man who, of all men has exercised the greatest influence upon the human race ... Muhammed.[33]

Washington Irving (1783–1859) – Well-known as the "first American man of letters":

> He was sober and abstemious in his diet, and a rigorous observer of fasts. He indulged in no magnificence of apparel, the ostentation of a petty mind; neither was his simplicity in dress affected, but the result of a real disregard to distinction from so trivial a source.

> ... In his private dealings he was just. He treated friends and strangers, the rich and poor, the powerful and the weak, with equity, and was beloved by the common people for the affability with which he received them, and listened to their complaints.

> ... His military triumphs awakened no pride nor vain glory, as they would have done had they been effected for selfish purposes. In the time of his greatest power he maintained the same simplicity of manners and appearance as in the days of his adversity. So far from affecting regal state, he was displeased if, on entering a room, any unusual testimonial of respect were shown him.[34]

---

33. John William Draper, A History of the Intellectual Development of Europe, vol. 1, (London: George Bell and Sons, 1875).
34. Washington Irving, Life of Mahomet (London: Henry G Bohn, 1889).

May Allah guide us all to the truth

Ameen